TALKABLE

Bio

Guy Richards is the founder and CEO of Abiah, an innovative brand development firm. A progressive speaker, blogger and strategist, Guy coined the term "Talkable" to describe his philosophy of building an irresistible brand from the inside out. He also pioneered the BrandReturn® Testing Methodology, which is revolutionizing the way organizations analyze their brands.

He has received numerous marketing and brand development awards, including four Davey Awards for Creative Brand Development and three Top 100 Global Rebrand Awards by ReBrand. Today, he takes a relational approach to research, strategy and design and specializes in developing and managing brands for Christian and value-based organizations.

Connect with Guy:
www.guyrichards.us / His blog
www.abiah.com / His work
@branddelight / Twitter

TOM,
KEEP PUSHING FOR
HIM!

TALKABLE

BUILDING YOUR BRAND FROM THE INSIDE OUT

Guy Richards

Eph. 3:5-6

To book Guy Richards for a speaking engagement, visit www.guyrichards.us.

FIRST EDITION

Creative Direction by www.abiah.com
Designed by Matt Gaylor
Photography by Bill Banks
Edited by Andrea Willits

ISBN 978-0-615-35635-8

Contents

Acknowledgments

I once heard someone say, "It takes a village to raise a child into a man." As I sat down and started looking back at all the people who have played a role in my life, I realized the weight of that statement. Through all the people who have reached their hand down to me, I can trace one common thread that leads to Jesus. And if it wasn't for Him being so kind to me, teaching me through the Bible and holding to His promises, I wouldn't care about much but myself and definitely would not be doing what I'm doing. For that, I'm grateful. He is my favorite teacher.

I have a wife who is super understanding to my time demands, encourages me and does a great job at making sure our kids, Brighton and Canyon, are at violin and swimming lessons, learn to ride their bikes and eat their veggies. I couldn't do what I do without her support.

I'm also grateful to the many others who have touched my life in profound ways. My dad who taught me how to strategically think and had me working by the age of 7. My (Italian) mom who still calls me almost every day to make sure I'm doing OK and eating well. My brothers Stephen, Brian and sister Katy who always inspire me to exceed my limits. My great grandmother in Ocean City who, in her broken English, would always warn me not to be "a busybody." My great grandmother in Linwood who modeled loyalty in marriage. My nanny in Somers Point who would fund all my crazy business ideas. My Candy pop who put his neck on the line to get me my first busboy job. My Nanny and Pop in Northfield who hired me at a young age and forgave me a lot. My in-laws, Rich and Carolann Klingert, for challenging my business methodology through the lens of chiropractic strategy.

My good friend Chris Einwechter who pushes me to believe God for things others would laugh at. Tim Chambers for telling me about Jesus in an interesting way. Aaron Campbell for giving me a foundation in the Bible. Lisa Price for teaching me structure. Winnie Anderson for giving me a great start in business and for helping BrandReturn® come alive. Ryan Burns for watering BrandReturn® and spending hours analyzing it with me. Phil DeAngelo for praying and inspiring me. Jerry Twombly for taking me under his wing. Bill Banks who answers the phone when I need help. Alan Bergstrom who taught me how to look at brand research in a whole new light. Johanna Sheridan who has become a catalyst of support and inspiration. Mike Duarte who shaped my technology strategy. Anaezi Modu who invested her knowledge in me when few were willing. Eric Spence who fanned the flames of my drive. My business consultant, Scott

Walker, who dedicated his schedule to cultivating me as a leader, strategist and business owner.

Finally, I'd like to thank all the other family, friends, clients and acquaintances who have shaped my knowledge and character and supported me.

Dedicated

This book is dedicated to all those who are passionate about the integrity of their word and the reputation of their brand name.

TALKABLE

Let's Get Started

Any brand that has become the benchmark of its industry is because it was or still is so unique that people can't help but to talk about it.

On the other hand, any brand that has become the example of a horrible product or service is because it was or is so awful that people can't help but to talk about it.

My name is Guy Richards, and I'm the CEO of Abiah, a brand development firm my wife and I founded out of our two-bedroom condo in 2004. I wrote this book to help you maximize the growth of your brand cheaply and organically, using an effective method called social strategy. *Talkable* is different from other books on the market because it's not a formula or an overnight success strategy. It's an intentional, time-tested, "slow-burn" approach for businesses that are really serious about sustainable growth.

In the pages ahead, I will thread one common theme: what it looks like to build a brand that people who are unpaid willingly advocate. That's right, building a brand that creates momentum from the inside out. I will first outline a testing methodology my team and I created called BrandReturn®, which will be the blueprint for you to uncover where you are and what it will take to move your business forward. Then we will go on a journey together. You'll learn 51 insights to create a brand that is positively Talkable and nine insights that drive me as a marketplace Jesus follower.

What does Jesus have to do with branding? Well, plenty. He plays a key role in leading and directing my everyday life as a businessman. Our relationship strengthens my commitment to exceeding standards of excellence and service—which then helps me achieve my goal of positive Talkability. So, don't be surprised if you're challenged to take another look at faith through a business lens. And if you're interested in meeting Jesus, I'd be happy to introduce you.

Enjoy!

—Guy Richards

The Foundation of Social Strategy

Social strategy is built from the idea that people have more influence on purchases and donations than a brand does in traditional advertising approaches (TV, print, Internet, etc.). That's because whether we acknowledge it or not, people talk. And what they say shapes how a brand is perceived.

There are only two ways to become Talkable. Deliver a great product and/or service to the market that no one else is doing. Or, deliver a horrible product and/or service to the market that everyone is doing.

The brand that falls in the middle of this continuum will become the clutter of the ordinary and be glossed over without a second thought.

It's rare for a brand to become successful from the inside out.

The reason it is so rare is because most brands are driven by leaders who are held accountable by a board to trim, pack and squeeze every ounce of profit from their current resources. This results in the destruction of employee engagement, customer loyalty and brand reputation, but in the short term, delights the shareholders.

I don't believe leaders make these decisions to destroy their brands. I believe they make these decisions because they're not offered or don't know of any other way. And the marketplace hasn't done a great job at promoting social strategies for the simple reason that an agency can't make that much money from this approach.

Yep, here lies the secret: Social strategy is the most cost-effective way to profitable, sustainable growth. And the reason it's not commonplace in the market is because a person like me, the CEO of a brand development firm, has to make a decision between:

A. Do we promote low-cost social strategies and tactics that yield the client a great return and loyalty but we don't make that much from?

Or

B. Do we promote high-cost tactics that yield the client an OK return and kill loyalty but we make more from?

As for me and my firm Abiah, we have decided to make an impact over profit.

Understanding Talkability

Positively Talkable brands have one thing in common: They create value from the inside out, which becomes contagious. First, it's felt internally, then it makes its way to the streets and builds momentum that energizes a group of advocates. That leads to dinner table conversations, Facebook and Twitter updates, blog posts, print headlines and TV critiques.

Everybody has an "influence group" they communicate with. This group is made up of friends, family, co-workers, acquaintances and those with common interests that a person has frequent contact with.

Think of people as explorers. Some take their job very seriously and others are casual, but we all work with the same goal, even if we do it subconsciously. The goal is to look for a brand that is great before the rest of the world knows it's great, and then share it with our group.

The prize for this is the esteem of the group for knowing something first, or the mental satisfaction that we have helped a friend in the right direction. On the other hand, we love to warn our friends to stay away from brands that we or someone we know has had a bad experience with. We do this to protect our friends, because deep down, we have an innate desire to help those within our group, and view people trying to get our money as people outside of our group.

"Influence groups" are so interconnected that their members start to become similar in the way they think and act. Here is a simple example: I was born, raised and still live in New Jersey. When I travel outside my state, it's common for people to joke about my accent. To me, I don't have an accent. People "down south" have an accent. Well, accent or not, the way I speak is a direct reflection of my influence group.

Before 2005, a person's "influence group" averaged about 40 people. But now, it averages about 300 people and is growing daily. This is because of the advent of daily social media interaction stemming from sites like Facebook, Twitter, Linkedin and others that allow the average person to communicate with mass amounts of people with a simple Send button.

If you have a small brand and small budget, scream for joy, because this is the only time in history that you have had the opportunity to exponentially grow within a small time frame as a result of becoming positively Talkable from social strategy.

If you have a large brand and large budget, grab your head, because this is the only time in history that you could exponentially shrink within a small time frame as a result of becoming negatively Talkable from traditional strategy.

When a brand is becoming Talkable, it's impacted in four stages. *See chart on next page.*

Positively Talkable	Negatively Talkable
Effect *When a person has a great experience with a brand, they tell about:* *Before 2005: 4 people* *Today: 300+ people*	**Effect** *When a person has a bad experience with a brand, they tell about:* *Before 2005: 13 people* *Today: 300+ people*
Aftereffect *The person who hears about their friend's experience then becomes influenced to view the brand in a positive way.*	**Aftereffect** *The person who hears about their friend's experience then becomes influenced to view the brand in a negative way.*
Momentum *The person then tells others about their friend's positive experience, which leads to awareness, positive perception and profitable sales.*	**Momentum** *The person then tells others about their friend's negative experience, which leads to negative awareness, negative perception and declining sales.*
Payoff *Brand increases profitability by decreasing its marketing dollars per customer/donor while riding the internal and external excitement of the market, which engages the staff to accelerate the cause.*	**Backlash** *Brand profitability decreases, employees feel the direct pain and become disengaged, the product and service quality drops and the brand slips into a downward spiral.*

Unpacking the BrandReturn® Testing Methodology

Every brand, whether for profit, nonprofit, small, medium or large, can use the BrandReturn® Testing Methodology to do three main things:

1. **Discover** which one of the four categories your brand is in.
2. **Forecast** the results or consequences that are in your near future.
3. **Strategize** a new plan to increase value and Talkability.

The History of BrandReturn®

In 2004, out of one of the two bedrooms in my condo my wife and I founded Abiah, a brand development firm. At that point I believed that if a brand looked good, it would become a great brand. At the time, I specialized in brand identity design. We had a small client selected to receive a Rebrand 100 Global Award by ReBrand and were showcased along with 24 Hour Fitness, Procter & Gamble – Zest, and Swiss Life.

But the thing that really convinced me that design trumped all else happened within Abiah's first 12 months in business. A startup that we led a brand initiative for, Surfing Artists International, caught the eye of multi-billion dollar company Bertelsmann, because of how we positioned them. Bertelsmann, known for investing in companies like Sony BMG and Random House Publishing, merged with my client. That gave Surfing Artists International a larger budget, which we allotted for a stronger marketing push. Then, in the same year, The McGaw Group, one of the world's largest print distribution companies, approached Surfing Artists International. The McGaw Group offered them an exclusive five-year agreement to wholesale their product in more than 60 countries and to more than 10,000 accounts. This would be The McGaw Group's second agreement like this. The first was with Disney.

Well, this really cemented my idea that brand design and marketing trumped all else.

But shortly after the excitement, the brand started to flounder. To my surprise, the same thing started happening with other clients. They would create initial momentum from external communications, but then they would slip back.

This challenged me to take a hard look at how I viewed brand initiatives. This honest assessment put me on a long road of researching and developing both small and large organizations.

Through my research, I developed a theory that is built on a simple comparison of Chiropractic vs. Medical Care.

Comparison:

In Chiropractic Care, the symptom of a headache is mainly addressed through the spine, which encapsulates a human's central nervous system. A disc in the spine shifts, placing pressure on the nerve, and the connection is shorted, which causes a headache. The chiropractor fixes this issue by adjusting the spine to relieve the pressure on the disc that is pinching the nerve.

In Medical Care, the symptom of a headache is mainly addressed through medication that masks the pain of the pinched nerve caused by the misaligned disc. In most cases, the medication quickly relieves the pain and deceives the patient into believing they are OK. After a period of time, the pinched nerve will resurface as a different symptom, like muscle fatigue or a sickness resulting from a compromised immune system.

I have found that unless the cause of any symptom is addressed, the problem will never be completely fixed. But most importantly, it won't sustain the strongest and most profitable growth, positive word-of-mouth—yes, Talkability.

Like the Medical Care industry, the majority of the advertising, marketing, public relations and branding industries approach projects from the same "quick fix" viewpoint. They address symptoms rather than the cause of the symptom, which stimulates enough short-term buzz to let them win the heart of their client for the project term. But this mentality compromises the brand's market perception, market loyalty and competitive position. That will then lead it into decline, because people either aren't talking about the brand or, even worse, talking negatively about it.

Test Your Brand

Out of my journey, my team and I created a proprietary testing methodology called BrandReturn® that identifies and traces the connection between the negative or seemingly unnoticeable symptoms of an organization to their fundamental internal or external breakdowns. This enables a brand's leadership to forecast the impact, lifecycle and competitive positioning of the brand being assessed.

Step 1 / Discover

Test your brand to identify which one of the four categories it falls into: Recreate, Reposition, Accelerate or Innovate.

1. Log on to **www.brandalignmenttest.com.**
2. Use your complimentary code **2TALKABLE6000.**
3. Answer the 18 questions.
4. Receive your score and learn your brand's health.

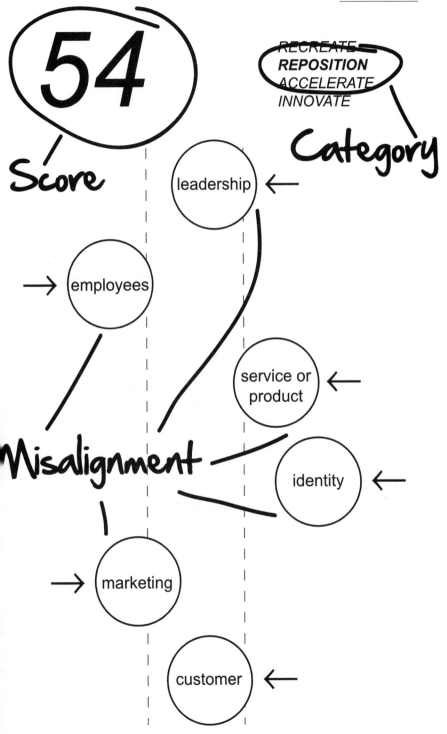

Step 2 / Forecast

Use the identification chart (below) to assess whether your brand is moving forward or backward. The symptoms of Regression and Progression listed from A- to L- and A+ to L+ will guide you.

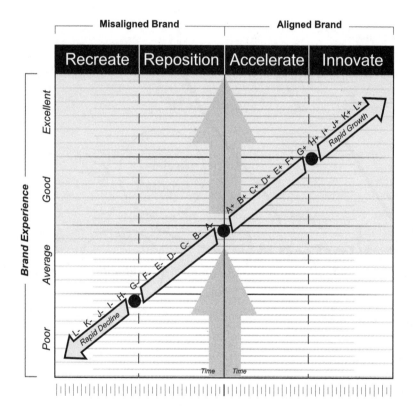

Misaligned - REGRESSION

A- Signs of decline are disregarded
B- Competition makes gains as distinctions blur
C- Budget declines, organization becomes price focused
D- Profit margins shrink
E- Attracts more price focused customers/donors
F- Value focused customers/donors leave
G- Better employees leave, performance declines
H- Quality of new hires declines, morale declines
I- Product/service quality drops
J- Bad buzz spreads, Brand Detractors grow
K- Brand Talkability becomes negative, value decreases
L- Organization is sold or goes out of business

Aligned - PROGRESSION

A+ Clarifies and adjusts the vision and mission
B+ Emphasizes unique promise of value
C+ Margins allow for growth
D+ Quantity increase, expenses decrease
E+ Attracts customers/donors who are value driven
F+ Customer/donor loyalty increases
G+ Higher quality applicants apply, get selected
H+ Lower skilled staff leave, improve, or are removed
I+ Product/service quality goes up
J+ Good buzz spreads; Brand Advocates created
K+ Brand Talkability becomes positive, value increases
L+ Organization further penetrates / expands offerings

The definitions below will help you get an idea of what your brand's category means.

Recreate: The brand has made wrong moves or remained stagnant for a period of time, and the market is unable to believe that the brand's service/product could be a value, even if the service/product did once have value. Brand leadership needs to address its value offering and recreate a new brand face including name, message and visual identity to establish a relevant platform to reengage the market.

Bottom Line: This brand is in rapid decline and is negatively Talkable.

Reposition: The brand's direction is blurred, the service/product is wrong or needs to be developed, the brand is internally misaligned, lacks appeal, possibly has the wrong audience and sends an unclear message. Brand leadership needs to develop a stronger strategy, appeal and value to catch the attention of or reengage the market.

Bottom Line: This brand is on the verge of rapid decline, and starting to become negatively Talkable.

Accelerate: The brand has a good plan, strong staff, a service/ product that provides value compared to competitors, and the right audience profile, but they are missing out on opportunities. Brand leadership needs to slightly adjust to reach or resonate with a larger market or new area.

Bottom Line: This brand is at a pivotal crossroads and is on the verge of being positively Talkable.

Innovate: The brand has a substantial hold on their segment's market share and preference. But as competition advances and market demands increase, it will be essential to consistently develop delivery, quality or service/product innovation to remain as a top performer.

Bottom Line: This brand is in a great position and is positively Talkable.

Step 3 / Strategy

The rest of this book is dedicated to challenging the way you think. The one common thread you will find throughout the following insights is how to create a brand from the inside out that will create waves in your market.

Feel free to read one insight a day or pound through them all today.

#1
Word-of-Mouth Influence (Your Best ROI)

There are many different ways to approach marketing campaigns—communicating the features, high-pressure sales, price build-ups, focusing on the pain and the list goes on and on.

But these tactics are useless unless you have a strategy of profitable sustainability. Most quick sales tactics leave customers feeling unimportant, misled and taken advantage of. This causes suspicion in the mind of your customer/donor that they are likely to share with someone.

An organization should never let their agency plan marketing campaigns until the agency explains the long-term repercussions of the plan. If an organization wants to have a positive reputation, it's up to the leadership to police their agency's tactics.

The challenge here is that we live in a world that demands quick results. Tricky tactics achieve fast results but only for a season, while shipwrecking the organization's future.

Sustainable Solution:
A positive reputation translates into a sustainable revenue stream. That's because a positive reputation wins people's loyalty and gets them advocating. And when advocacy starts, sales/donations are at their purest form while increasing profitability.

There are two reasons most organizations don't invest in their reputation:
1. They don't know how.
2. The glitz of quick revenue wins priority.

#2
Brand Advocacy (Common Sense and Street Smarts)

The *Brand Advocate and the **Brand Detractor are one and the same. What action ensues depends on the experiences they have with a brand. You can identify these individuals by two main traits: common sense and street smarts.

Common sense allows a person to determine if the brand's service, product or cause is something that's needed or was created from an isolated opinion.

An example of an isolated opinion without a lot of common sense would be trying to sell canned oxygen to people in Australia because the CEO had a dream the country would be the first place to run out of air. The company's motive may be pure, but their common sense is lacking.

Street smarts is being able to discern whether the motive behind the brand's action is for the greater good or self-pleasing.

These days, we have millions of organizations jumping on the philanthropy business model. To me this says, "We like to make money. If you will give us your money because we share a little, we will do that. Because hey, we will do anything for money."

A pure motive with a high level of common sense creates advocacy, which leads to loyalty.

On the other hand, either the wrong motive or low common sense creates a group of people who will make it their job to deter others from the brand.

*Brand Advocate: One who attracts people to a brand.
**Brand Detractor: One who deters people from a brand.

#3
When You Feel the Pain

Your skin doesn't sting when you don't have a cut, but when you have a cut, even water makes it hurt. The problem most organizations run into is not identifying core problems until it hurts—and by then, it's too late.

Yes, we all run to the immediate need like a surface cut. But the more important issues that steamroll organizations, like value offerings, customer service and internal cohesion, are not usually realized until a large symptom appears. By that time, the problem is so out of control that it can take multiple years to correct. That's assuming you find the right external group(s) to handle it, because you only get a short window of opportunity to turn around a brand in decline.

Most organizations track employee time charts, some sort of quality control and complaints/returns. But very few have peeled the onion down to the first layer. What I mean is, they probably have internal damage, but until they feel the pain, they won't do anything about it.

If an organization cut back the things they monitor to the most important ones that all others stem from, they would literally be six months to two years ahead of most of their competitors.

Tracking core issues takes a new mindset and good use of historical data to set realistic, forecasted goals. But the main change the leadership will find is the ability to manage employees by results, not time. In order to do this, employees need to have a clear picture of what you want them to achieve.

#4
Brands Inspire Belief

A brand inspires belief in a forecasted future. The belief works as a solution to a problem. The greater the problem, the more engaging the brand will be.

A quick insight:
Money is not a solution, nor does it inspire belief. Money is a by-product of a great cause. If you are solely driven by profit, you will most likely succeed, but you will have a disengaged staff and a lethargic, transient client base.

I'm not saying profitability isn't important. Planning your organization for sustainability insures your cause. But the cause should not be replaced by profit...if you want to inspire advocacy.

#5
The Art of Measurement

What do we measure? Everything!

We measure how our day is going by our previous experiences of great days we've had. Interbrand measures the **Top 100 Global Brands** and Outreach magazine measures the **Top 100 Fastest-Growing Churches**. Every measurement taken has a reference point of worst and best, even if the lines are a little blurry.

It's really simple. Some people will say, "Well, at least I'm not as bad as…" while others stay in the middle of the indicators, hoping not to stir the pot.

But then, there are those who are not satisfied with the worst- and best-case scenario. These people have an internal drive that is far greater than the drive of those around them. They set their own standard of "GREAT," which the world has yet to see.

It's only when a gifted visionary can paint the canvas of "GREAT" that "GREAT" can be achieved. Which pushes the bar of best-case scenario forever.

No longer do the innovations of the competition cause the visionary business owner to fret. It's because the measurement this person is using is so far ahead of the standard that they are looking to God for what is possible.

What is your life's measurement standard? Or is it hard to explain because it's so far past best that you are redefining the standard daily?

#6
Ground Zero

Have you ever measured your plans against eternity? I mean, after this life and on to the next?

Or do your plans stop at retirement or death in this life?

When a person realizes that this life is an arena that determines their eternal dwelling, their definition of success should change. This then redefines their goals and plans.

I'm a person who believes that after this life, everyone ends up in one of two places: heaven or hell. And the final destination is determined by one thing: *Have you asked Jesus Christ to forgive your sins and be the Lord of your life?*

Because of my belief, I have a choice. I can coast through this life being quiet so I don't offend anyone, or I can step up and use the resources and time I have left to help others spend eternity with God in heaven.

The second choice is hard! I will be criticized and mocked by others who think what I believe is made up, and in some circles, I may become a social outcast. But if I don't speak up, despite believing that every person, no matter how good they are, will go to hell if they don't ask Jesus Christ to forgive them and be their Lord, I'm a hypocrite. It's like a fireman who won't save a person from a burning building because he doesn't want to offend her by picking her up.

Do your plans stop in this life?

#7
Design Without Value

I have had my hand in about seventy five rebrands in the last 5 years. What I see time and time again is design without value.

The purpose of redesigning a brandmark (logo), marketing material, ad campaigns and a Web site should be to catch the eye of the media and consumer to communicate value over the competitors. It also reinvigorates employees to be proud of the place where they work and sends the message, "Yes, we are relevant and growing." But if no distinctive value is being offered behind the hype, then you still have an ordinary product that no one will talk about.

Soon the buzz of the new design will fade, and the company will be worse off than when they started.

#8
The Business of Brand Recognition

In the beginning of 2009, Tropicana, who has invested years into brand recognition, redesigned their visual identity. The new brandmark was less readable. Consumers didn't recognize it as Tropicana and sales fell. Soon, leadership realized the redesign was a bad idea and scrapped it.

This company could have saved a lot of face, plus millions of dollars in execution, if they identified that their value was in product recognition.

People shopping for a product are likely to compare brands once. After that, the buying decision becomes mindless and they "do what they have always done."

Don't skip discovery and strategy, or execution will cost more than you want to pay.

#9
What Does Nike Sell?

Before I answer this, I'll tell you what they don't sell. They don't sell sneakers, socks or sports apparel. If you said, "What? I'm wearing Nike sneakers now," give me a few sentences to explain.

Nike sells athletic ability and victory.

If you pay attention to Nike commercials, you will find that they don't talk about how long the laces last, the manufacturing of the soles or the durability of the leather.

Instead, they emotionally connect to the deep inner drive we were created with to push past our limits to achieve something great. What you will see on Nike commercials is a group of kids in the streets playing ball with a stick for the love of the game, a basketball player hitting a three on the buzzer to win the championship, or the look of determination on the early morning runner's face as she blazes through town.

The tangible product or service we all sell is the catalyst that addresses the deeper emotional need.

These days, the stakes are too high to sell product features. Average people (like me) now have a voice that reaches the masses, vast fields of competition are entering the market every day, and online shopping is driving prices down and demanding service be at its best.

Do what you love, and do what you do with passion. People who do what they love create great brands.

#10
Competitors!?

You compete even if you don't want to. Your business prospects will get second and third estimates or use your model numbers to make online comparisons.

I have found two ways most business leaders handle competitors:

1. Ignore them.
These business leaders build walls around what they listen to and view. They focus on the production of their product/service with great intensity, hoping to maintain a steady margin. The problem with this is that one day, the brand's leadership will wake up and realize that 40% of their customers have switched to their competitor. This happens because of a market innovation, price point or new delivery option that the business leader would have been aware of months or even years before, if they had just observed their competitors.

2. Become consumed with them.

These business owners are so focused on every detail of what their competitors do that they start looking alike, speaking alike and marketing alike. Subconsciously, they believe that what their main competitors are doing is right, and they fear being left behind. The problem with this approach is that it positions the brand as a follower, not a leader. That position is nearly impossible to get out of once the marketplace picks up on it.

I have found both of these viewpoints to be unsuccessful. The best way to handle competition is not from an "ignorance" or "jealousy" standpoint, but rather as an observer. An observer knows who he is, is confident in his character and purpose in life and uses what's around him as gold nuggets of opportunity to fast track his purpose. He doesn't get caught in "jealousy" of his competitors' success or in "ignorance" of them, but wisely uses them as marketplace indicators like the orange buoys on a river way.

An observer learns from his competitors' "New Coke" failures, which allows him to maximize his R&D (research & development) department and adjust his structure. He is a doctor monitoring the health of his market through the symptoms of his competitors.

#11
Branding States (Three License Plates / Three Value Statements)

Distinguishing your brand or even a state in a few words is a challenge because it's usually hard for the leadership to pick one statement to communicate.

Common methodology for deciding what to communicate:

1. We need to let people know what we do.
     Minnesota – "10,000 Lakes" (We do lakes.)

2. We need to let people know what we have done.
     North Carolina - "First in Flight" (We were innovative.)

3. We need to let people know how we think.
     New Hampshire – "Live Free or Die" (We live fearless.)

These methods are common, but not right in every situation.

Here's a strategy I use that works well. First, identify the group of people that is "adamant" about what you sell. Then define how they think, and why what you sell is a part of their lifestyle. This group is the trendsetters.

When you figure that out, you can start to identify what this group sees as value when buying, associating or linking their cart to yours.

Pick only the top three things they value, then prioritize them in order of importance.

Minnesota's trendsetters' prioritized values may be:
1. Secluded fishing
2. Open waterways
3. Lakefront property

Once you have this information, you can position your core message and offerings.

P.S. It may sound weird, but I have found that positioning your brand to your trendsetters will insure a wider reach with less "cost-per-sale." Your trendsetters only make up about 10% of your market, but the majority of the other 90% seem to follow.

I have no hard facts on these numbers, just my experience.

#12
How to Use Social Media (your .com, blog and Twitter account)

Think of your blog as your "Sunday best face," and your Twitter account like your "weekday face." OK, I hope you don't have a church face and an "everything else face," but hopefully you get the picture.

Our culture craves authenticity, because it is so rare today. So people stand in the corners watching from a distance, hoping to find proof that what you say on your blog, business site or stage is who you really are when you let your hair down.

Three things to remember:

1. Your business site is where you offer marketplace value and showcase your results.

2. Your blog is where you create innovative thought leadership.

3. Your Twitter and Facebook accounts are where you interact as a real human.

Not much room for error these days, because the world has never had a better magnifying glass than the Internet to search for authenticity.

PLAY BALL!

#13
Purpose

I have to admit, I had a lot of fear of the unknown growing up. I asked questions like, "Why was I born? Why wasn't I born into a wealthy family? Why am I so skinny that people can see the ribs in my chest?"

And the most important question I asked was, "What is life about?" We have no choice in being born. We also have no choice in when we die. If you can't relate to these questions, then disregard what I'm saying. But if you can relate, let me share with you.

You are created with a specific purpose! Unfortunately, I don't know what that is, but I can point you to the One who will tell you.

"For I know the plans I have for you," declares the LORD, "plans to prosper you and not to harm you, plans to give you hope and a future." (Jeremiah 29:11 NIV)

God also said, "You will seek me and find me when you seek me with all your heart." (Jeremiah 29:13 NIV)

The insight is that God said this, and God can't lie. Because if He did, that would mean He couldn't be God because the title "God" itself means to be perfect.

So, if you seek and ask with authenticity, He will answer, or you can dismiss both of us as liars.

P.S. I once cursed God out; yes, the F-word was a part of it. I couldn't get over the fact that God would let this much pain into the world. But what I didn't realize at the time was that He didn't want to create robots that love Him because they are forced to. That would not be love but control. Love is offering someone a choice.

#14
Social Media...New Tool, Old Strategy

The strategy of leveraging audiences hasn't changed because of social media. But how it's done has. Or, I should say, who draws the audiences has changed. When Larry King, Jay Leno or the trade industry you belong to needs a guest or a keynote speaker, this is how they make the decision.

Choices:
A. OK Speaker + OK Content = Huge Audience
B. Great Speaker + Great Content = Tiny Audience

Eighty percent of the time leadership will choose A, because a huge audience means more people, higher ratings and increased revenue. About 20% of the time, the gatekeepers will be kind and bring in a person who has a heart-wrenching story—you know, one of those bootstrap-to-glory tearjerkers.

Yes, times have changed. Reality TV has taken over glossy,

flossy actors and Twitter is allowing the average person to gain a following that will soon be comparable to Oprah's.

But the one thing that hasn't changed is this simple equation: Person + Huge Audience = Stage.

The advent of social media is like watching the dice in Yahtzee bouncing around, not sure how they will fall. Strategy will always stay the same; we are really just watching tactics change!

#15
The Little Blue Box

What can we learn from that little blue box? It has starred in movies, made women crazy, and left men empty-pocketed.

Tiffany & Co. knows something! They know that people buy with their hearts more than their heads. This retailer has built a perception of luxury through every consumer touch point.

They have created an experience that makes the consumer feel like a millionaire, even if they shoveled snow all week to buy an $85 Mesh Ring for their girlfriend. (Yes, many years back in college this was my story. She is now my wife.)

What matters are the stories we tell ourselves and the feelings we associate with the things we purchase. Who do you know who wouldn't want the best of the best if you took price out of the conversation?

In all reality, what Tiffany & Co. is selling is not jewelry, but a lifestyle, status and confidence. The statement from a man to a woman is, "I love you enough to give you the best" (which isn't always true). The jewelry is just the symbol of the feelings being sold.

#16
Strategizing Opportunity in a Market Shift

Every market innovates, and therefore, causes businesses to adapt their offerings and delivery.

It's no surprise that On Demand TV is putting a lot of video rental stores out of business.

Brick-and-mortar video rental stores' "costs-to-operate" usually consumes 80% to 90% of what they make (that is without the competition of On Demand TV). So, if On Demand TV takes 30% of the video stores' sales, they are 10% to 20% behind on their bills. This puts the video store in a race to decrease costs before the wave of floating overhead crashes.

A great example of taking advantage of a market shift is Redbox, the self-serve DVD kiosks. The strategists behind Redbox identified that there was still a market for video rental, but delivery would have to be drastically recreated. And they did it.

Redbox figured out how to eliminate labor, cut rent and negotiate with supermarkets to insure traffic positioning while eliminating marketing costs. Now, they can offer rentals at a super low price, $1 per day, and still be profitable.

Here are three questions to help you identify opportunity in your market:

1. What out-of-the-box idea would allow you to eliminate or greatly decrease fixed costs while increasing profitable, long-term growth?

2. What is the potential risk and reward?

3. Where will you be in three, five and 10 years if you don't change?

#17
Can a Small Business Build a Brand?

I often hear the question, "Can a small business build a brand?" The truth of the matter is, every organization has a brand. The question should be, "How does a small organization leverage its brand?"

If you focus on delivering excellence to your market (defined by your market's viewpoint), you will be growing your brand. You don't need a flashy logo, matching stationery or a Twitter account. These are not bad things, but for every organization, across every industry, the primary component of building a strong brand is providing more value than your competitors.

In the area I live, you can ask almost any local for a great sub shop and, out of the thousands, they will point you to either Sugar Hill Subs or White House.

They both have great subs, but still have flaws. Their signage is not much better than a mom-and-pop shop. Inside they are both laid out like small delis, and the employees are not in uniforms, but they are not building a reputation on anything other than what they do best...delicious subs.

Yes, they may be able to expand their market and accelerate their reputation through more relevant marketing and design, but they are still the best without it.

It doesn't matter if you are Al's Pizza or AT&T. If your service or product can out-deliver your market's top competitors, your reputation/brand will grow.

#18
Be Clear About Your Brand Promise

Most leaders understand what a brand promise is, but to recap, a brand promise is the claim of distinction made to the market. The more value the promise has, the harder it is to deliver, but if you can deliver, your organization will get more market favor in comparison to your competitors.

Examples:
Fedex - The World on Time
Toms - One for One
BMW - The Ultimate Driving Machine
Target - Expect More. Pay Less.
Compassion - Helping release children from poverty in Jesus' name

These brands have stuck their necks out with their claims. They have connected with the market and have been able to deliver on their promises, accelerating them as market leaders.

Whether you're in ministry, business or government—small, medium or large—here are four brand promise principles to accelerate you:

1. A brand promise creates a plan
The primary purpose of a brand promise is to tip customers/ donors in your favor. The secondary purpose is to inspire your team to push industry boundaries, which creates engagement and inspiration.

2. No promise, no standard
Not having a brand promise is comparable to having a bad one. Without a brand promise, there is no organizational standard to live up to. That places you in the ordinary category from the customer's/donor's perspective and creates internal disengagement.

3. A brand promise aligns unspoken market needs
The claim you make should be something your market is craving (and sometimes, not necessarily asking for) and competitors are having trouble delivering.

4. Deliver, deliver and deliver
The hardest part of any promise is keeping it. Over-promise and under-delivery are the main reasons organizations fail. There is a saying, "Great marketing will put an average business under."

Know what your cause is, know what you're competing for, know your competitive rank and build a plan to offer and deliver the best.

#19
The Fork in the Road

The other day I was reading about Jesus crying as He looked at Jerusalem. He said, "They will crush you to the ground, and your children with you. Your enemies will not leave a single stone in place, because you have rejected the opportunity God offered you." (Luke 19:44 NLT)

Isn't that crazy? God, who can do whatever He wants, decided to come down in the form of a human and offer His people an opportunity. He didn't control them or force them to make a decision. He simply offered an opportunity, and was in tears when they made the wrong decision.

I'm on the journey like you, but here are three things I do when I'm faced with a fork-in-the-road decision:

1. Ask God to give me wisdom, insight and discernment, and ask what decision He thinks I should make (I should say, "know I should make"—He is God). I believe James 1:5: "If you need wisdom—if you want to know what God wants you to do—ask Him, and he will gladly tell you. He will not resent your asking."

2. Determine the motives behind the decision I want to make. This helps me minimize emotion blurring my choices.

3. Err on the side that will make God smile. This does not mean safety. This means quitting an advertising job when I was asked to design a Reef ad (known for girls in thongs). Or confronting a boss on ethics.

Here is the first part of that verse: "But as they came closer to Jerusalem and Jesus saw the city ahead, He began to cry. 'I wish that even today you would find the way of peace. But now it is too late, and peace is hidden from you.'" (Luke 19:41-42 NLT)

Yep, they lost the opportunity, but even scarier, they won the consequence.

Make sure you carefully consider your opportunities…you will have to live with them forever!

#20
The Glass Sales Pitch

I received a call from a company that sets up networking meetings between brand development firms and large brands looking to hire.

The sales representative told me that we (Abiah) were hand-selected by a team of experts who believed we were a great match for this group of brands. He went on to explain how successful this opportunity would make Abiah.

Then he revealed the cost: $35,000. He backed it up by explaining how each brand had at least $100 million in sales, $5 million for marketing and had signed an agreement to launch four new projects in the next nine months.

It didn't make much sense to me because I knew I would have to compete with larger and better-staffed organizations. In my experience, the more bodies in the office equal a higher level of confidence to mega corporate brands.

I thought about it and said to the sales representative, "If you are so confident that I would be successful at your event, would you work out an agreement with me to only pay you if I win a contract? I'm willing to pay you $70,000 (twice what you want) assuming I win a contract."

Needless to say, he declined. Funny how some people are so confident you will succeed until they are asked to put their money where their mouth is. If this sales representative was so confident I would succeed, he would have at least told me he would ask his manager.

I guess the pitch was as fragile as glass.

#21
Proud to Know Brand Ordinary!?

There is an emotional prize in being associated with a brand that is great before the rest of the world knows it's great.

People thrive off the esteem that they knew about X before you did.

But I have never heard of someone who passionately claimed that they knew about a brand that was ordinary.

#22
Leadership Integrity
(Brand Perception and Reality)

I have witnessed a lot of erosion in brands due to a leader's words not matching his actions. It's such a simple equation, but extremely hard to deliver.

Passion + Claim of Distinction + Delivery = Trust

Or

Passion + Claim of Distinction + Under Delivery = Distrust

People who...

Trust you: are loyal, recruit their friends and advocate for your cause.

Or

Distrust you: are hurt, don't come back and persuade their friends not to select you.

As a leader, your brand's perception and reality starts and ends with you. What is the end result you want?

#23
Found Treasure

What if you found a treasure that was so great, so unique and so large that you could not keep it all to yourself?

That's right, you would tell a friend how to get some.

So, what do you sell again?

#24
Defining Your Market's Thought Process

Every market has decision drivers. Here is a simple test to determine if your market is made of short-term thinkers (minimal or no vision), long-term thinkers (vision) or a blend of both.

If a segment of your market buys the cheapest (insert your product or service here), they are probably short-term thinkers.

If a segment of your market buys the more expensive (insert your product or service here) that lasts longer, they are probably long-term thinkers.

If a segment of your market buys the "super, super, hey look at me" (insert your product or service here), there is a good chance they are short-term thinkers.

#25
How to Teach

Have you ever had a teacher who seemed to get pleasure from using words that should require a license to use?

I'm not the best at classroom learning. In fact, I'm pretty bad. I repeated 7th grade and was in the lowest classes possible in my high school. By senior year, I was down to two academic classes, gym and graphic design, and I was out before lunch.

But on the other hand, if a teacher illustrated while teaching, or tied the lesson into a story, I could repeat it frontward, backward and remember the temperature of the room I was in when they said it.

I came across this passage years back that has stuck with me.

"A wise teacher's words spur students to action and emphasize important truths." (Ecclesiastes 12:11 NLT)

Everyone is a teacher at some point in the day or week. If only 15% of what we teach with words will stick with those we are teaching, we need to find new methods, even if it means teaching over banana splits.

It takes love to step outside of our comfortable ways to connect with others. And love is what opens doors and crosses boundaries to illustrate what words can never do alone.

P.S. God could have just saved us with words. But instead He decided to illustrate His point of love by allowing Himself to be brutally beaten by His creation, besides taking the penalty of the sin of those who put their faith in Him. What a great lesson, taught by a great teacher.

#26
Primary Message –
Pain, Health or Inspiration?

Most marketing messages in a bad economy focus on pain, whereas in a prosperous economy they focus on health.

The reason is because most people can't see past their toes when things are bad, or when fear creeps in. But when things are good or seem to be, the road ahead is in clear perspective.

It's like my friend Bobb Biehl says, "Imagine if a world-class body builder nicked off the tip of his pinky finger. What do you think his focus would be on? This little piece of his body that, reasonably stated, doesn't mean much to his everyday life? Or, the body-building event of the century that he has worked his whole life for that takes place in a week?"

I believe it's just better to inspire rather than use fear to motivate sales! Who is with me?

#27
Three Things Your Staff Must Do

Here are three things to ask your staff to deliver on:

1. Acknowledge every prospect/customer/donor even if you can't help them right away. Even if it's just eye contact, a facial expression or a head nod.

2. Say something.
This forces the staff to be creative.

3. Inspire.
Give your staff the freedom to go out of their way to bring joy to those who choose to use you.

I once heard a story about a woman who asked for milk for her infant at a sports stadium food bar. The young man asked where the lady was sitting. He then ran outside the stadium to a convenience store and purchased the milk, warmed it up and brought it to the mom.

The woman was so impressed that she decided to inspire him by sending a letter to the stadium's leadership.

Why not lead the way in your market? It doesn't really cost that much more.

#28
Brand Vs. Bottom-line Focused Organizations

From my experience, I believe there are two kinds of organizations: "brand-focused organizations" and "bottom-line focused organizations."

These two mindsets lead to two very different outcomes.

Bottom-line Focused Organization
The bottom-line focused organization's primary concern is here and now. They think, "How can we profit the most off every transaction, even if we have to use pressure to squeeze the last penny out of a customer/donor?"

This organization will soon go under or fade into the background of the market as a result of disappointed customers/donors sharing their experience with friends and family (and these days, on Facebook and forums).

Brand-Focused Organization
The brand-focused organization's main goal is a great reputation that drives profitable sustainability. They think, "How can we please our customers/donors by consistently giving them a great service/product and an unexpected experience, even if we financially break even in some situations?"

This organization will slowly build a great brand reputation and secure a top position in the market, while sustaining the loyalty of a base of advocates who will not consider another option.

What is the focus of the organization you work for, want to work for, lead or do business with?

#29
Stuck in the Boardroom

I have found that many great ideas are bottlenecked in the boardroom for three main reasons:

Limited Perspective
The board is too close to understand the reality of the outside perception of the organization. Because of their limited perspective, new strategies are built in a chamber around the individual likes of the board, not what will work best for the organization.

The Hobbyists
Most boards are filled with decorated individuals who are highly respected, but don't necessarily have a reason to turn a profit. Hence, they are known for dragging out decisions, which sends a message to stakeholders that the organization is just ordinary.

The Undercover Strategist

Most boards have one or more people who want to be the hero with the great ideas. These individuals are known for dragging out agendas, and are the reason most meetings last hours past the scheduled time.

All three of these challenges can only be fixed through a great chairman or outside consultant who is willing to be hated for a short time.

#30
Your Reach in the World

I know six CEOs who have determined they have an influence on 100,000 people through their positions in life.

They identified this by the effect their decisions have on others (employees, customers, vendors etc.).

You may be a stay-at-home mom who has two children, leads a book club and is a roller derby coach on Friday nights.

Or,

a single guy living at home who is in design school, works as a bike messenger and plays the bass in a band that does covers on the weekends.

Either way, your life is specifically positioned with the people around you. You may have many years with these people, or just a few hours left. But the real question is, *"How are you impacting them today?"*

#31
One Life...One Opportunity

"There was a rich man who was dressed in purple and fine linen and lived in luxury every day. At his gate was laid a beggar named Lazarus, covered with sores and longing to eat what fell from the rich man's table. Even the dogs came and licked his sores.

"The time came when the beggar died and the angels carried him to Abraham's side. The rich man also died and was buried. In hell, where he was in torment, he looked up and saw Abraham far away with Lazarus by his side. So he called to him, 'Father Abraham, have pity on me and send Lazarus to dip the tip of his finger in water and cool my tongue, because I am in agony in this fire.'

"But Abraham replied, 'Son, remember that in your lifetime you received your good things, while Lazarus received bad things, but now he is comforted here and you are in agony. And besides all this, between us and you a great chasm has been fixed, so that those who want to go from here to you cannot, nor can anyone cross over from there to us.'

"He answered, 'Then I beg you, father, send Lazarus to my father's house, for I have five brothers. Let him warn them, so that they will not also come to this place of torment.' "

"Abraham replied, 'They have Moses and the Prophets; let them listen to them.' "

" 'No, father Abraham,' he said, 'but if someone from the dead goes to them, they will repent.' "

"He said to him, 'If they do not listen to Moses and the Prophets, they will not be convinced even if someone rises from the dead.' " (Luke 16:19-31 NIV)

Jesus answered, "I am the way and the truth and the life. No one comes to the Father except through me." (John 14:6 NIV)

That if you confess with your mouth, "Jesus is Lord," and believe in your heart that God raised him from the dead, you will be saved. For it is with your heart that you believe and are justified, and it is with your mouth that you confess and are saved. (Romans 10:9-10 NIV)

As a businessperson, you have only one opportunity to serve those around you and make a difference in the workplace. Make your life count.

#32
Relationship Stress
(Brand and Consumer)

When the relationship between brand and consumer/donor becomes stressful, only three things can happen:

Break up: This will damage not only the individual relationship, but also future ones with those who hear about the breakup. The other downfall is that when a breakup happens, whole groups of people never find out about the brand through the word-of-mouth of the consumer/donor.

Accept it: This causes the problem to build inside the consumer/donor until something triggers an explosion. Then, there is a high likelihood of the person speaking negatively about the brand at an accelerated rate.

Reconcile: This usually happens when the brand makes a mistake and takes responsibility for it. (I wish I had customers who said they were wrong and asked to make it right.) The brand then decides that fixing the issues, no matter what the costs, is in its best interest. If the brand errs once or twice, it usually causes the consumer/donor to talk highly of the brand. If errors happen on a repeated basis, it will lead to a "breakup."

The proactive approach is to build systems to avoid error, but even the best brands will make mistakes. Plan B should be to handle them better than anyone else.

#33
Calibrated By Purpose

It's easy to veer off course toward every speck that glitters on the horizon when you don't have one main priority that calibrates the direction of your brand.

Just like a pilot who sees a brilliant sunset or a majestic mountain range in the distance can be persuaded to drift off course to see their beauty, even a person with a goal can get off track and lose time coming back.

If you believe your brand has a purpose and you know what it is, it's critical not to get sidetracked, even by possibilities that seem attractive and promising. Opportunity is just that—it's here for a minute and vanishes.

#34
Gimmick = Give It to Me Now!

Brands that succeed are built from character, not gimmicks.

Character is built on dreams and conviction.

Gimmicks are built from a desire for more...now.

#35
Shaping the World Starts With YOU!

Culture is adapted from micro-movements, and micro-movements are created by storytellers, artists, musicians, motocross riders, programmers, dancers and snowboarders.

Like a small spark that sets a rainforest ablaze, these movements commonly start with one small thing—unhired leaders with a hatred for the ordinary and a passion to tweak the style that identifies a group of programmers, dancers or snowboarders.

Think of all the male skaterboarders who started wearing tight girl's pants years ago. Then, it was just a few. Now it is common practice for the mainstream.

P.S. Culture is not created by rules; culture is not created by legislation; culture is not created by the majority. It's started by YOU, the one who just can't take what the rest of the world is settling for.

#36
Culture and Money
(Creating Positive Brand Culture)

Does money really have the power to attract the best employees?

Well, it depends on how you define "best." I define best as fully engaged in the purpose of the brand, highly talented and an inspiration to be around (introvert or extrovert).

I find that these employees are motivated by purpose and value… in short, a positive culture. Being highly paid is a plus.

On the other hand, a brand can pay very well but have a poisonous culture and bad employees. I define bad as disengaged in the brand's purpose, on an ego trip and being a person that people want to run from.

Yesterday I had a friend say, "I left that other place to work at this place. It doesn't pay as much, but I'm happy."

Purpose, joy and inspiration are an effort to maintain, but anyone is capable of possessing them.

#37
Gifted for Business

I have come across a perception that seems to follow Christian business people. The perception is that we are not as holy as those who are in full-time ministry.

I have wrestled with this on occasion, but I have no desire to be a pastor. I love business, I love ministry, but more importantly, I love ministering in business. I love being a light with the skills I have been given in brand development and social strategy.

Let me share something with you that came right from the red words, yep, Jesus' lips.

"I tell you, use your worldly resources to benefit others and make friends. In this way, your generosity stores up a reward for you in heaven." (Luke: 16:9 NLT)

This may sound weird but I want to share it:

I love making money for business owners.
I love analyzing competitive weakness, strengths and
opportunities.
I love building strategies to increase my client's market share.
I love design, for no other reason than style at times.

These activities allow me to use the gifts I have been given to win people's trust and favor, which gives me their ear to talk about Jesus (or increases resources for Kingdom work). And sharing that Jesus can set souls free is my favorite thing. It makes me complete.

I'm not sure why God has built me with these seemingly weird but complimentary gifts. But like a runner was built to run with the speed that God gave Him, which makes Him smile, so I thrive because I feel at home in this realm.

The moral of this rant is that God has created you as a businessperson, yes, as a Christian businessperson, and He doesn't want you to walk with your head low because you can't find an example of the gifts you have in anyone you know. Remember, God builds unique people for unique times.

Trust Him and focus on what you have been given to make Jesus known...while there is time left.

#38
Be Careful With the Word Yes!

Yes is a dangerous word when it involves organizations being put in a position that exceeds their ability. Because if an organization doesn't deliver according to the expectations set, they will leave people on the receiving end disappointed.

The quickest fall for a brand starts with a disappointment.

On the other hand, when a brand stays in its circle of ability, it increases its delivery and impresses people, and those people tell others. Then the organization slowly but strongly grows.

#39
Mr. Startup

Don't trade longevity for velocity.

The biggest lie I bought into is that we as startups have to come out with guns blazing, using 100% of our resources to make a splash upfront.

Time and time again, I have witnessed startups go out of business because of this strategy. They buy into the idea that they can build a reputation overnight that will drive sustainable margins. To their demise, resources dry up and they are back looking for a job.

Velocity is not a bad thing if you have the capital. But unfortunately, most of us don't have unlimited resources.

The best bet for any organization is not to trade longevity for velocity. Focus on relationships, let those relationships build and make delivering trust a priority.

Big businesses have been built as a result of longevity. Chick-fil-A was started in a converted home, and McDonald's first built a great reputation off one stand.

What was that saying about Rome...?

#40
The Passion of the Leader's Vision

How a leader views the cause of the organization greatly determines its success.

I have found that when a leader has passion and urgency to reach the brand goal and his/her lifestyle and actions align with the cause, it creates an organizational rally. The excitement motivates the leadership that motivates the employees, which overflows to the clients/donor base.

Your brand's loyalty, both internally and externally, will always be a direct reflection of how the leader portrays the cause... good or bad.

#41
Invisible Line

There is a burden that only leaders can understand…an invisible line that, once it's crossed, you can never go back.

To cross the line means you have an opportunity to make a great impact, but it also means that those you lead will view you differently. They will not understand your full responsibility or all the reasons you make decisions. They will suspect you have it easy, not understanding that you're probably up most nights thinking how to minimize the burden of others.

For those who have crossed the invisible line, I commend you; leadership is not all glamour as most non-leaders view it. But you know that.

I have found that the best way to engage those on the other side of the invisible line is to be intentional with your unspoken communications.

1. If you're traveling with an employee and there is one bed, sleep on the floor.

2. If you have a Snickers, offer to share it (for real), then give away the bigger half.

3. If you have to make a hard decision, be the first to sacrifice.

These simple actions will be the roots of reaching the movement's cause. But you will have to care about reaching the cause more than you care about your comfort.

#42
Chaos and Gaps

When the leader is physically or emotionally absent, chaos runs wild.

I heard a story about a mom who would leave her three young daughters home for days on end. There was not just physical neglect but emotional. The lady had about 17 children from who knows how many men. During the mother's absence, one of the daughters who was about 8 drowned her infant sister.

Could the young girl's mind have been so warped by her mother's neglect that she thought she was protecting her young sister from the pain? I don't know.

But what I do know is that this could have been avoided if the mother was physically and emotionally invested in her children.

This is an eye-opening correlation for CEOs, managers, and in fact, anyone. When we as leaders invest guidance in those coming up the ranks, we cause hope and inspiration. When we neglect to share our knowledge and time, we leave gaps.

#43
Seed Planter /
Marketplace Ministry

This insight is for the Christian business owner. What if you decided to use your business to make an eternal impact?

OK, so you sell pizzas, car parts or widgets. That means you have resources, customers, vendors and maybe employees that you influence.

You are a steward of something that is unique, special and rare. Business owners who are based in the United States make up about 1.4% of the U.S. population. And being a "Christian" business owner, you probably make up .25% of the population.

Being rare is good, because God is always on the lookout to show His power through unlikely individuals who want His agenda.

"The eyes of the LORD run to and fro throughout the whole

earth, to show Himself strong on behalf of those whose heart is loyal to Him." (2 Chronicles 16:9 NKJV)

You have been entrusted with seeds; you can eat them, keep them in a locked safe or replant them and get to experience a multiplied harvest that has eternal rewards.

Why not use your business to influence others to spend eternity with God?

A great example of marketplace ministry is In-N-Out Burger, a well-established fast food restaurant on the West Coast that places Bible verses on their cups and burger wrappers. Or Forever 21, a popular fashion clothing company that prints John 3:16 on the bottom of their bags.

These are just a few ways you can have an eternal influence. Be creative!

#44
Don't Wait for the Right...

If you wait for the perfect time, staff or number in your savings account to move forward, you will always be hindered. Leading requires risk, or, I should say, faith.

#45
The Social Mores of Brand Culture

Social mores are not rules, but undefined social codes of conduct that a culture lives by. They are things the government can't punish you for, but the people who belong to various cultural groups can.

It could be picking your nose at your family's get-togethers, or going the wrong way on an escalator in Macy's.

Social mores are prevalent in strong brand cultures. Imagine if a new Apple executive owned a Blackberry, or an employee at Tom's shoes wore Nike's. How long do you think they would last?

From a follower standpoint: What if a Honda rider wore a Harley jacket, or a fan wore a tie-dye Grateful Dead shirt to a Jay-Z show?

The stronger the brand culture, the more social punishment you receive for breaking the group's social mores…and the group's social mores are set by the depth of the leadership's conviction of their values.

Weak conviction = weak culture.

#46
Scent Branding

Great brands tap into all five senses—sound, sight, touch, taste and smell—to create an emotional connection with their market.

The major sense that is least used and the hardest to leverage is smell. But yesterday my wife noticed a brand that has done an excellent job at it. Babies"R"Us is now placing scent on their gift cards.

What a great idea. It makes women's pocketbooks smell great and triggers a memory connection that keeps the brand in the forefront of the mind. In my wife's mind, Babies"R"Us will be bookmarked for years to come as the innovator of this idea.

Innovative ideas win "shelf life" in the mind, and increased margins follow.

#47
Small Business...
Get to the Trusted Friend!

My friend Bill is a one-man-show with *two* businesses. He is both a photographer (Bill Banks Photography) and a computer technician (Advanced Users).

The other day he was venting and explained how he was on a photo shoot and noticed that the company's computers were not set up properly. He questioned the company about them, and the owner said, "I know they are wrong; I just don't have the right people."

Unfortunately, that business owner didn't have people he could trust, people to tell him what to do when he didn't know.

Bill has a saying he tells his clients. "Have people in your life that *know*, that you can trust, so you can hear what they say and do what they say."

Bill understands the key to a great company-to-customer/ donor relationship is...trust! And in most industries, trust is a competitive advantage because so few companies value it or work to establish it.

Educating your clients builds trust that leads to a relationship built on a strong foundation. Your customer's advocacy will eventually spill over and secure your growth.

#48
Excitement and Bad Decisions

When decisions have to be made, leaders tend to weigh the pros and cons.

I would challenge that method to say, when a leader is making a decision, a key factor should be the "team's excitement."

I will make bad decisions on purpose (from others' perspective) if it means making my team excited. That's because I understand that team engagement is driven by excitement. What I mean is, say I make a decision to spend more money than necessary to benefit the team, some could look at that as a wasted resource. But I look at it as a future investment in human resources. People know when you care about them. It is shown by your actions.

A team that knows they are loved is more engaged.

I know this isn't what the majority of marketers would

suggest because it doesn't sell for much and won't reap an instant return, but it will lead to a great reputation and profitable sustainability.

#49
God and Your Employees

I was praying one day and these words came out, "God, allow my desires to be Your desires so I will be a better husband, which will make me a better dad, which will allow me to live the purpose You have set for me."

It then made me think about how employees' motives affect their companies.

What if your employees worked to please God?
Your employees would want God's desires to be their desires, which would cultivate a great work ethic, which would increase your product quality and service delivery, which would please your customers and drive better brand performance, which would accelerate your organization in reaching its goals.

What if your employees worked to please themselves?
Your employees would want to take the easiest possible route,

which would make them do the minimum to reach the maximum results, which would decrease your product quality and service delivery, which would be the catalyst for losing customers, which would place your organization in an uphill fight for survival.

#50
Organized Brands Win

Have you ever found yourself looking for a rare item or service? The process goes like this: 1) Google the rare item, 2) find a list of possibilities, 3) call the possibilities, 4) and finally, compare value.

Even if you're not looking for a rare item or service, but it's your first time talking to a brand you have never purchased from, you may find yourself in a bad conversation like this:

You: Do you sell X?

Brand: Well...let me ask my manager. We can do that.

You: Have you ever done this before?

Brand: Yeah, lots of times.

People don't have much confidence in a brand that doesn't have a structured service/product offering. The only way an unorganized brand can compete is on price or turnaround time.

This problem is prevalent in young and aging organizations. Young organizations are trying to get their feet wet, find their sweet spot and develop their skills. Aging organizations get stuck in their processes that once made them great, but miss the fact that their competitors have increased the value of their offerings and the market has become more demanding.

Live life with your market, shop your competitors and define your offerings. Say "NO" to good things and "YES" to great things. Only then can your brand build a reputation that will travel first class, via word-of-mouth.

#51
Positioning Statements

Do you know the best way to come up with a positioning statement?

Get groups of average people in a room and observe how they communicate with each other about a specific product, service, or brand. Once you find common themes that describe value in down-to-earth terms, you can boil the information down into a short statement.

That's how The Richards Group came up with The Salvation Army's new "DOING THE MOST GOOD" campaign that helped them increase their budget in a down economy and how H&R Block became a hit a few years back with the "I got people" campaign.

#52
OK Then,
Dress Your Baby Boy in Pink!

I sometimes find myself in debates about design and color with business leaders who can't seem to understand how design and color are tied to emotion and can be harnessed to impact profitability.

I thought of this argument to illustrate the point.

Dear business leader and father, if color is meaningless, dress your baby boy in pink. If design is meaningless, dress your baby boy in a dress.

#53
The Value of the Antagonist

Anything worth achieving has someone, something, or a group of someones and somethings standing in the way. But you must hurdle these problems to achieve the vision you set out to complete.

Opposition is the great catalyst of community movements. It gives the community a reason to stick together.

I have heard people say, "Tell me what you're for, not against." This is good because you should never lose focus on your cause, but even this statement communicates that you are against something. Why else would you be stating you're for something unless there was a problem?

The goal for the community is just as much the process of being against something as it is achieving the vision.

#54
Consistent, Unique and Relevant, or Clutter of the Ordinary

Consistent, unique and relevant are the three characteristics that make up a brand that people positively talk about.

If you lose one, it all falls apart. It's like a man I know who always wears a bowtie. He is consistent in wearing them. It is unique because people rarely wear them anymore, but it's not relevant.

At the end of the day, if this man were a brand, he would fall into the "clutter of the ordinary" category between being positively talked about and negatively talked about.

In short, it becomes something we see but pass by.

#55
The 86-Year-Old Lady

I was running out to drop off a box at the post office and grab lunch. Before I left the office, I asked God for an opportunity to tell someone about Jesus.

I wanted to get a frosty at Wendy's, but God directed me to this little mom-and-pop deli that I haven't eaten at in years. I parked and decided to take my Bible in. When I made it inside, I noticed there were only four people in the whole deli, and two were behind the counter. The other two were an 86-year-old lady and a man who didn't seem up for talking.

I decided I would tell the older lady who seemed very kind to "walk with the Lord" while I was walking out. I paid for my sandwich and told the lady, "Walk with the Lord." But she was trying to say something to me and didn't hear me.

I got out the door and heard God say, "Go back in." I was so scared. I stood there for a few minutes and told God that I trusted He would give me the words once I went back in the deli, but I needed the courage to walk back in.

At this point, I was consumed with what the people inside would think about me if I went back in, but having been in this situation many times before, I decided to trust God and walked back in. While I was walking in the door, I heard God say, "Sit down and eat with her," but I was scared and went to the bar at the window instead. I took my jacket off, then pushed past the fear and went to the lady's table and asked if I could eat with her. She happily let me. She even said how great it would be to eat with a young man.

She cleared some room, I sat down and we started chatting. While she was talking, I asked God for an opportunity to share what He wanted with her. She then told me how her husband had died and she wasn't sure if she was going to heaven.

I opened my Bible, read and then explained Romans 10:9-10 (NIV). *"If you confess with your mouth that Jesus is Lord and believe in your heart that God raised him from the dead, you will be saved. For it is by believing in your heart that you are made right with God, and it is by confessing with your mouth that you are saved."*

Can you believe how God can use someone who is so scared?

#56
Movement Recipe / The Blind Side

I watched an interview on 20/20 with the husband and wife who took the now-NFL Baltimore Ravens player, Michael Oher, in when he was 15 and homeless. The recent movie The Blind Side tells their story.

The 20/20 interviewer asked a question that grabbed me: "Who benefited more, your family or Michael Oher?" Mrs. Tuohy quickly responded, "We did." She went on to explain how their house was always buzzing with people who wanted to help. She described it as "communal."

My mind quickly broke this up into a classic portrayal of a great movement:
Michael Oher: The cause
Mrs. Tuohy: The champion (leader) of the cause
The school: The support team
The goal: A better life

Once a champion grabs onto a cause, it has a higher likelihood of succeeding, because there are lines of people waiting to follow something great. God put it in our veins.

It's a really simple equation: The greater the cause + the more challenging the effort + the greater the leader backing it = the more engaged people are to help.

Sign me up!
P.S. Movements are rarely preplanned.

#57
Branding Begins in the Mind!

People like some things worn, like snowboard boots, and some things new, like sandpaper.

Either way, there is a mindset behind why people buy that is usually ultra-different from what the brand perceives.

Brands that can court a tribe are the ones that dive into the culture and subconscious mind of their consumers to find out how to tailor their product or service to get the best word-of-mouth traction.

Nike is known for athletic products, yet they have a department that studies the mind of the non-athletic culture and designs custom shoes for the purpose of style, not performance.

This approach has proved extremely successful for the Nike brand. Demand for their custom shoes has created a group of people called "sneakerheads" who will spend a few thousand dollars on an older pair.

The strategy is to create a demand that increases your main market while opening new markets.

#58
Sorry...Only One Message Per Brand

In a shaky economy, brands try crazy things. Make sure you understand the risks of character permission if you are thinking of extending your offerings under the same brand name.

Big brand, small brand, or individual, everyone only gets one message per brand.

It would be a failed attempt if Sony, who is known for technology, announced they would be using their brand name to expand into the diaper business.

Say you had a friend who was a hippie who followed Phish around. One day he came to you wearing saggy pants, talked with the "I want to be a rapper voice" and told you his new favorite artist was Jay-Z. Would you take him seriously? (That made me laugh)

Businesses can branch out, but depending on the offering, it may require establishing a new brand. Procter and Gamble is a master at this. They own Tide and Duracell. Tide can't sell batteries and Duracell can't sell laundry detergent.

Make sure your brand has the character permission of the market if you are thinking of expanding.

#59
Consumer Multiplication

How a consumer feels about your product, service, and brand is more important than the particular item they buy.

People may never remember what they purchased from you, but they will remember how they felt when they purchased it.

The more positive the feelings, the better your chances that referrals and purchases will multiply.

#60
Impact List

Every great leader who has used their position to positively influence those around them is a by-product of someone.

These are the rare people, ones who, when they speak, empower others to push past their own boundaries.

These people are not necessarily rich or influential in culture but are willing to stand for what they believe, even in the face of opposition. They are the ones who say what they mean and mean what they say.

I know that time is a resource in high demand. So I'll be quick.

1. Grab the closest piece of paper to you.

2. Think of those friends, pastors, authors, relatives, etc., who have had a positive influence on your life.

3. Write their names, titles and how they played a part in the person you are today.

Now share the results with a close friend, and enjoy the memories. Chances are, you are on someone else's list because of the people on your list.

Conclusion

One thought drives me when I teach: *"Because the teacher was wise, he taught the people everything he knew...and he did so in an interesting way."* (Ecclesiastes 12:9a-10 NLT)

In this book, I've done my best to teach you everything I know, and I've made it as interesting as possible. But you know what? Knowledge isn't everything. I thought long and hard about the most important thing I can leave you with, and here it is.

I believe that action is more important than knowledge. Because knowledge can be piled up to the heights of hoarding, and unless it is utilized through action, it's worthless. On the other hand, someone can lack knowledge but start out on a path of action, and through their experience, gain knowledge.

Now that you know where your brand stands—whether you're regressing or progressing—and have been spurred on by the progressive strategies in this book...it's time to take action.

What are three things that will get you where you want to be, that you can start today?

1.

2.

3.

Today's date:
The date you would like to arrive:

Notes

The Business of Brand Recognition (page 33)
1. Elliot, Stuart. "Tropicana Discovers Some Buyers Are Passionate About Packaging." The New York Times. 22 February 2009. http://www.nytimes.com/2009/02/23/business/media/23adcol.html?_r=1

Seed Planter / Marketplace Ministry (page 93)
2. "Statistics about Business Size (including Small Business) from the U.S. Census Bureau." U.S. Census Bureau. 4 September 2008. http://www.census.gov/epcd/www/smallbus.html
3. "U.S. POPClock Projection." U.S. Census Bureau. 31 August 2009. http://www.census.gov/population/www/popclockus.html

Branding Begins in the Mind! (page 115)
4. Brown, Anika. "Sneakerheads Come Clean." Wiretap. 8 June 2009. http://www.wiretapmag.org/arts/44248/

TALKABLE